MORNING BOUQUET

GAUTAM MRIDHA

Made with ♥ on the Notion Press Platform
www.notionpress.com

Life is made of small incidents, a moment of joy, a moment of sorrow, a moment of loneliness, a moment of sharing and many other minutely detailed minutes. I dedicate my work to my parents, my family and all the friends whose loving care gave me such a beautiful world to live in.

Contents

Contents

Mother to Daughter

Text messages sent by you in millions
cannot replace the voice of your dear,
but just a minute phone call could
make me happy and near.

Habit changing

Facebook is like a deep fridge
you opened minutes earlier,
still, you wish to try again
expecting delicious deliveries
kept there by some name.

Talking to you

I prefer to be an active listener
better than remaining a passive talker,
it is then easy to visualize
Curls of your hair before your eyes.

The millions of syllables
gushing out through the pebbles
just like a frolicking stream
never stop even in my dream.

I pick up your emotions,
A drifting boat in the ocean,
you laugh and then you cry,
Fearing the black cloud of the sky.

Chattering to the friend
finally comes to an end,
All those magic moments
stored with the words spoken.

Innocence of the creator

Tarry a little, look up at the sky

Even in your busy runabout,

I will tell you why,

Don't you see the creator ? ...

The One, never tired of writing,

Staging dramas of every kind.

Appreciate his innocence,

making potteries floating high,

rabbits & birds out of nothing

none of them are ever alike.

Creating them in dozens of white,

shading them with grey or coloured dye

Occasionally lighting them up with the silver lining,

Decorating them with a rainbow tie.

Nature salutes with smiles of flowers

Birds with their chirping,

I offer my mute prayer

Thanking you for your caring.

books of different kinds

once upon a time, it was my life
Reading novels of every type,
Be it Gorky Agatha Robin Conan Doyle
Arthur Premchand Sarat Bankim.

Sharing thoughts with the writer
I had spent many afternoons together
Now I read words of a different kind
The civilisation which was lost long ago in time,

Reading clues for their existence
left as the signature of one presence,
I search them in millions of pebbles
inside mounds of huge rubbles,
The scene waiting to be traced again
just as a hologram out of the time machine.

These objects reveal the creative mind
and the knowledge those people left behind.
Footprints are often left in the past
engraved in the stone forever to last,

Feel them in the temple of Petra
see them in the rock at Bhimbhetka,
hidden among the rubbish of mohenjo daro's

Sign of wisdom of those long-lost heroes.

A lone sparrow

A lone sparrow sitting on the fence

Wondering what shall he do

build a nest and wait for a companion?

Or hop from tree to tree in the wood.

Nature prefers him to settle

His heart wants to move abound

See places and make new friends

Unveil mysteries all around.

Watching him from a distance

Another one tip-toed near

"Never seen you collecting grains

And the winter is not so far ?"

Reality broke the morning silence

Heart overruled by unfriendly brain

Mind stored the wish in memory

Commanding the body to do tasks with pain.

Wish, the lone sparrow had a company

One who would also fly too

Accompanying him from place to place

Share the joy of knowing new.

You were a celebrity

Surrounded by a band of friend

you were always a queen bee,

I used to admire your locks

your eyes were as green as the sea.

you excel in everything

studies, debate, drama, and dance.

compare to that I had nothing

no scope left for any romance.

You smell of cinnamon

Voice as sweet as honey

Keeping everyone mesmerised

always made the climate sunny.

I tried to steal a glance

In the school year after year

you kept your head high

I adored you from far dear.

Three decades of summer gone

You were a princess in my memory,

My childhood flashed back to yesterday

Hearing "Don't you recognise me ?"

Your Soul

The soul is like a butterfly

just transforms but never die

Doing its duty it disappears

Carrying pollen flowers to flowers.

You may feel sometime

a stranger in your lifetime

Someone you met in life train

rings a bell in your brain.

The soul recognises each other

Your heart needs to decide further,

You may forget to remember past block

Just return the smile

let the soul talk.

Family

Just a kid of ten years I was

out of the shadow of dad and mom

not to blame the destiny, but

both wanted , to be on my own.

That day,

You were hiding away your face

So gloomy it was, still

You were assuring me of all niceties

Which would follow when I complete.

Never missed any Sundays

You travelled miles and miles

Turn by turn , for long six years

brought me always basket of smiles.

You taught me tolerance,

The meaning of a ‘family’

relation growing on respect and sacrifice

Just not limited to bro, sis, dad and granny.

I shall carry your message

Take it to the next century,

Shall coexist with nature

Leave in peace and harmony.

Sacred garden

You could hide your sorrows,
Below your eyelids,
You could keep your smiles,
Between your lips,
Happiness and Joy you could
Hide from others,
To share with the dear ones,
Should you hide your emotions,
Within your kind heart of yours,
Lo behold, it will grow securely
as a bunch of daffodils,
In the sacred garden of love of yours.

Silence

Silence may give you peace,
Silence may give you happiness,
While amid your running,
But silence kills me slowly,
As I am at the end of the race,
Kindly pray for me,
Silent forever I will be.

waving your lights

I am like a ship
floating endlessly in a lonely sea,
you are a lighthouse
standing to affirm on the ground.
I see the faint light
from far away
guiding me always
back to the coast.
And when I return
I see you always
waving your lights like a lovely smile.

Light and shade

A thin line separates light & shade
Happiness & sorrow are two sides,
Nothing Nature like us to avoid,
Need to learn to exist with smiles.

Your smile even in your hardships,
Encourages me to outwit mine,
My challenges to my difficulties,
Feel easier, when you say a line.
All of us live for each other
Sharing joy and sorrow,
Respecting the rule of nature,
Hoping for a better tomorrow .
In days of bitter and better
We always remain together
Listening to inner voices
Sharing thoughts and choices,
Ray of hope shining in the sky
Nothing could be better to try.

Listening to you

I always liked to listen to you,
Rather than talking,
You preferred hearing me,
I could speak nothing.
While you were looking in the mirror,
busy am I reading books,
Should have said then just,
"How pretty do you look".

Time travel

I have travelled through times for million of years,
to know you,
I have crossed seven rivers and mountains
just to see you,
I have spent years after years, days and nights.
just to meet you,
Even then I am not at all tired
and shall
still, be Loving you.

walking together

For many many decades
basking in my den,
sleeping with arrogance
stoning my heart to death.
A new dawn arrived in the lull,
it had its colour and hue,
vibrant laughter lingers on the wall,
delicate like a drop of morning dew.
I saw the night and the stars,
through million pairs of eyes,
the kindness beneath them,
strong but resilient like skies.
I have crossed the last few steps,
Knowing cannot walk together,
keeping deep in my heart,
promise to love all of you forever.

women in me

I never believed the women in me,
the first joy of missing the month,
the first visit to the clinic,
the first Doppler scan, and the shadow,
the resemblance to a new beginning,
and the assurance of the long wait,
I fell instantly in love with it,
the thing I have never met,
the flower blossoming,
changing slowly me into a new me
forever.

whisper a few words

You inspired me
to be the better part of me,
you applied your special herb,
whenever you see my injured heart,
your flash of a smile,
lights up my mind,
even if I wish,
I can give you nothing of my own,
just because,
it is already been yours,
I, therefore, place a rose,
before thee,
sometimes when I am not around,
pick it up and whisper,
a few words for me.

my wish

To me,
You are a world unexplored,
every moment I see a new light,
a new beginning,
and there is a lot to learn more about.
you carry the mystery as in the universe,
reveal a little here and there,
I know you, or may not.
What I see in your twinkling bright eyes,
a little bit of old over new.
I feel you when you sit alone at Times,
I like when you toss your rays over the clouds
there is an awe in you,
Maybe that is why I wish to know you.

Travelling miles

My eyelids seem heavy,
not due to lack of sleep,
they carry the memory,
of loving bond brewed during the trip.
Watched the vastness,
so overwhelming,
rustic green-grey wilderness,
so enchanting,
white Rabbits in the sky,
keep floating,
Skyscrapers near and high,
so nestling.

Shining cars race by,
on six-lane whispering shy,
Humanity of colours
living in harmony,
respecting dignity,
of everybody.

Saw lazy sunset
painting rainbow twilight's,

on the slanted hill so deserted
gentle Pacific washing feet.

Twelve days went by,
seems to be now a dream,
watching birds and butterfly
sharing nature's spoil as a team.
We have driven mile after mile,
capturing tons of memories,
preening heart making a promise,
return before my eyes die.

Feme America

Whatever it may be,
Feminine America looks to me.
trees are draped in
million coloured pin,
Blue skies
resemble eyes,
long trees like high boots
walking tall on green pastures,
canyon peaks,
painted nails,
vast uncharted land
just like a girls hand.

Orionid shower

I felt like an alien always,
from a place far away,
might be Regel or Betelgeus.
Tonight look up at the sky,
you may receive a letter,
through the Orionid meteorite.
A sweet word to melt your heart,
for a precious few moments,
you wished to receive long ago.

missing you

You provided me to build in me
Perfect scientific temperament,
You carried me over your shoulder
To see the circus of elephants.
You ran behind me
To teach cycling,
Coloured the canvas,
For Rainbow painting.
This world I see
Through your eyes,
But now wearing your shoes
I miss your advice at every step.

Loneliness

Loneliness is like a high heel shoe,
a single misplaced high tempered brat,
sitting silently in a corner locker,
patiently waiting for a pickup.
Day and night, listening to the same beat,
the day has gone when she used to shine,
with a loving and caring hand,
stomping on the road head held high.
The dearie has become prettier,
she needs something better,
a new model, a new trendy fashion,
the old one has been offloaded to the bench.
Even now the pair is strong,
Sitting silently at the locker,
They look eagerly at the dearie,
will she put them on?

my thoughts

I am just like anyone should be,
I like to laugh to run around playing
I run behind butterflies and honey bees
just to see them flying.
I love listening to your story,
the real things from your life,
they seem like dreams to me.
Floating softly in front of my eyes.
A picture behind the mirror,
just like a piece of my dream,
she was always, there
only I failed to see.
As independent as she could be,
she paints her colour,
the same spirit she shows,
while love and care.

mobworm

There was a time,
reading every dime,
in black and white,
and feel the writer's chime.
Decipher the thoughts
with families and friends,
cry or laugh it out then,
on mindful of glorious words.

Now bookworm meta morphed,
mob worm as they are told,
they read silently,
they watch silently,
whether standing or seating,
working or cooking,
bathing or even sleeping.
Reading through their fingers,
twitching the eyes never,
a few mad smiles here and there,
keeping only to himself, whatsoever.

warmth of your heart

When I peep into your heart,
I see a pretty pink little room,
two windows on the wall,
one of them in a golden frame,
let you see the world,
the way it wants it,
another window smaller one,
much higher eye level,
wants you to see the world,
the way you want to see it.

The smaller window
hiding from everyone,
brings your warmth in cold winter,
moonlight washes down,
I survive in the warmth of your heart,
Only you can feel me out.

In dry summer or a cold winter bright,
a shiny day or a stormy night,
I would always wait for you there,
for your caring hand, with mittens a pair.

I see you everywhere,
I see you in everyone,
I feel you in the air I breathe,
Just let the hair go down, I can see it.

Let the cloud give you shade,
Let the rain give you cool,
I shall give warmth to your heart,
to spread the message of love.

dreaming

When you will be sleeping,
I would come to you on tiptoe,
and softly whisper before your ear,
you are my little one, don't you know.

you are in your dreams,
I shall wake you up never,
you are always in my dreams
no one else except you could enter.

In there, I live with thee,
by the north sea where the sky shines,
you would be busy making clouds,
I could help you make rain.

Be in my dream when you can,
but never go away thee,
touch me with your soul,
when I feel lon

best friends

Be it summer or winter,
a stormy night or a windy day,
in the hours of joy
and hours of sorrow,
Be my best friend always,
you can hit me,
pounce me,
laugh me,
joke me,
cry to me if you want to,
but my shoulders will be
always there for You.

I bleed my strength
minute by minute,
second by second,
when I stay apart from you,
Still, I love to take the pain,
of staying afar and bleeding,
as some day somewhere
We shall meet together,
may a few lightyears ahead.

oneness

I
and you
have one soul
when born in womb
drew apart while we grew
like other sides of the mirror
you see the world with your spectacles
judging based on what you have then learnt
then grey years sets you to unlearn many things
till you realize you and me are nothing but one .

eternal sleep

A king Wished,
wise man Planned, a sheer Determination,
Muscles of thousands, and Support of millions,
years and years of Toiling, behind the quietly Flowing dawn,
manmade miracle Happening, Shaping a wonder for eternity,
withstanding in awe in time.

Finally a site
set to a time of sand rustling
beside the Nile flowing
king sleeps in peace & eternity
with all the elegance and purity
to wake up sometime in the future
for another day and another ledger.

Printed by Libri Plureos GmbH in Hamburg,
Germany